I0620190

Love, Faith, & Bullets

Love, Faith, & Bullets

My Unspoken Sermon

Nathan Wells

ARPress
ILLUMINATING IDEAS
EMPOWERING VOICES

Copyright © 2023 by Nathan Wells

All rights reserved. No part of this publication may be reproduced, distributed, or transmitted in any form or by any means, including photocopying, recording, or other electronic or mechanical methods, without the prior written permission of the copyright owner and the publisher, except in the case of brief quotations embodied in critical reviews and certain other noncommercial uses permitted by copyright law. For permission requests, write to the publisher, addressed "Attention: Permissions Coordinator," at the address below.

ARPress
45 Dan Road Suite 5
Canton MA 02021

Hotline: 1(888) 821-0229
Fax: 1(508) 545-7580

Ordering Information:

Quantity sales. Special discounts are available on quantity purchases by corporations, associations, and others. For details, contact the publisher at the address above.

Printed in the United States of America.

ISBN-13:   Paperback   979-8-89330-797-9
                eBook   979-8-89330-798-6

Library of Congress Control Number: 2024904453

Preface

This is a series of poems telling the story of a young Christian black man's life. This string of love notes, family, war, and soul searching describes the inner thoughts of how an honorable US Air Force Airman views the world around him. Deep within these descriptive narratives you will emotionally connect to life struggles of the southern Louisiana gentleman. You must read the poem "Speak Your Unspoken Sermon" to gather the true meaning of what is meant by unspoken sermon.

Nathan Wells is an active duty Air Force officer. The views expressed are the personal views of the author and do not represent the official views of the U.S. Air Force or the Department of Defense. If you would like to respond to the author, you can reach him directly via his Facebook page at

https://www.facebook.com/natebeanieunspokensermon/ (@natebeanieunspokensermon).

Acknowledgements

I would like to acknowledge those specific people who helped with making this book of poems a reality. I do not claim to be an outstanding poet but through faith, I pray that this simple book can touch someone as writing these poems has helped me through the years. First, I would like to acknowledge my father, Albert E. Wells, for placing the initial thoughts to place my collection of poems into a book. Thank you for always encouraging and believing in me. Secondly, I would like to thank Arabia Littlejohn for being the final push I needed to make this book a reality. Your belief in me, in my writing, and a game plan to make it work is exactly what I needed at a time when I felt alone and uninspired. A huge overwhelming thank you must go to my editor, Adrianne Cobb. Thanks for taking the time for going over every detail of this body of work to make it the best publication it can be. Long ago, when we were just mere teenagers, it was your poems that encouraged me to keep writing. You were really the first person outside of my family to tell me that my writings were good, and that I should share them with the world. A beautiful applause and thank you must go to my photographer for capturing the essence of each poem through her photogenic lenses. Next, I must give thanks to every individual in my life that had some influence in my life to the inspiration of these poems. Every poem is ultimately created from God, but majority of these poems had some influence from personal experience and sincere love for a significant person in my life at the time. Some of these individuals know who they are, and which poems were specifically about them so thank you to all of you. Lastly but not least, I must acknowledge my beautiful rock, queen, and helpmate, Felicia Wells, for being my happy ever after inspiration and cheerleading me on as I tackle my dreams.

Contents

CHAPTER THREE
MILITARY LIFE

CHAPTER FOUR
LESSONS & MEMORIES

CHAPTER FIVE
SHORT STORIES

CHAPTER ONE

Love Notes

These poems speak to every individual on the planet. It is a story told over the centuries time and time again, and never ceases to captivate the human heart. That is the story of love and heartbreak. Let's explore what true beauty looks like.

V-Day 2015

Good morning to thy love,
Who provides
... the sweetest of hugs.

Good morning to thy love,
My sugar dove,
...Kisses of electric buzz.

Good morning thy love,
My perfect sanctuary,
... Stomach with butterflies
Ecstasy in your thighs
- flows the juices of blueberries.

Good morning love,
My heart's key,
.... Security in thy purity,
Portrait of holy harmony,
My olive branch of peace.

Good morning,
The smell of apple pie,
Always on my side,
Willing to ride or die,
In me pumps your blood,
of family,
and soon to be.

Good morning, Valentines,
Will thy be mine?
And I thine?
And all there is to be?

Good morning to thy love,
who provides the sweetest of hugs.

Good morning to thy love,
My sugar dove with kisses of electric buzz.

Good morning thy love,
My perfect sanctuary,
…Stomach with butterflies,
Ecstasy in your thighs-
with your juices I soar the skies.

Good morning love,
My heart's key secured in thy purity,
Portrait of holy harmony,
My olive branch of peace.

Good morning,
My apple pie whose always by my side,
willing to ride or die;
In you pumps our blood of family and soon we will be.

Good morning my Valentine!
Will you be mine?
And I thine?
And all there is to be?

ALCOHOLIC

Sensual aroma of Bourbon
Mixed with the juices of your berries
An illustrious brown glow
Sitting in an ice-cold glass of perfection
The perfect blend of grace, beauty, and savagery
Devour enemies with her sex appeal
Befriending gentle souls with southern kindness

I take a sip
Mmmm
That delicious smoothness of her skin
Touching the ripples of my throat
Igniting torches in the chambers of my chest
I FEEL ALIVE
Alive With liquid courage to conquer the world
Lost in a delirium, walking shakingly
I never want this feeling to end
For I am addicted to this Bourbon
Because she is all I have, she is all I need
I love my Bourbon and she loves me
Never will I leave thee, for she is a part of me
Engulfed in the essence of all that is, Bourbon

Sip after sip, after sip
I cannot stop
I want more and more and more
Causing havoc to get to it
Sipping without care
Sipping without...
Any care what happens to me
Destroy all ties with my family
Nothing else matters....
As long as I have my Bourbon

Drowning in this state of total bliss
Pass out with sweet dreams of thy warmth
Wake up with a hangover, aching for more Bourbon

YOU

There is no tomorrow without the scent of your hair. Your presence is the present on Christmas morning. And the past is filled with the running memory of your skin smoothing out the edges of mine.

We lay against the moonlight night, a reflection of your beauty. The nightly mistress who sings sweet nothings into my ear enticing me into her bossism, warming my spirit with the aged wine of her love. As we connect the biological puzzles, no other piece fits more perfectly. Tearing my soul limb from limb with the exuberance of her passion my heart aches to catch up. I dare not stop as there is no desire to let go of the euphoria that is your skin. Only something God could have ordained which is the miracle of heaven placed here on earth. I only cease to move in the rhythmic pattern of this delicious lullaby is due to my human limits. But my true love far exceeds these limitations and transcends into the golden gates of heaven where this sensational feeling is never halted but only swallowed down into my belly until it is once again ready to excrete back into my physical form of perspiration and high of pure bliss

FALLING FOR LOVE

Falling, falling in-and-out of love
never out, only in
there's only one real way to fall.

Suckered punched by life
didn't see it coming
this unusual feeling.

Never contrived before
Outside, outside of family, religion, and friendship
but of the opposite sex.

Of some woman I've grown to know
cherished, upheld, and put on a pedestal
an angel of God.

Lust- spiritual, mental, physical- emotions
Overwhelming the
Ve-ry
Essence of thy be-ing.

I – LOVE – YOU
those three little words
can't be spoken out loud.

AFRAID! afraid she won't accept them
afraid she won't feel them
she won't repeat them.

They leave my breathe
can't turn back
forever gone in the wind.

Fallen on deaf ears
ears that refuse to hear
ears that won't neurotically transmit.

To the brain
to signify the mouth
to spit the message out - it just received.

Shaking head, no
mouth closed, shut tight
in disbelief.

Runaway; run away from the topic
never to return
these days together, are now numbered.

Once you Love
you don't Love another
never the same as you Loved that specific other.

Sure, someone else may come along
i may Love again
but never the way I Loved that specific friend.

She took a piece of me
never to be replaced
she forever holds the key to that closed gate.

Love is a tricky thing

it would make a man go crazy
envy, hatred, overwhelming joy and peace
sadness and deep sorrow, happiness, and ultimate bliss
make a man do things he never thought to do
feel things a man doesn't want to feel
behave in a manner beyond his own understanding
Love is a tricky thing
Love and Logic
don't really go hand in hand
to choose logic, is the smarter man
but choose love, is hu-man
Love is a tricky thing.

Yet I still look out
into that big blue sea
for that unique prize especially made for me.

Waiting on True Love
Love that last throughout eternity
a special bond that can't be broken so easily.

True Love goes through it all
the struggles, the pains, the hurts and flames
the ups and downs, high and lows, poor or fame.
True Love knows no bounds
it cannot reach, it sees
beyond the physical, material, and into the very spiritual - of thy soul.

Haven't given up
just waiting
waiting on that incomparable gift God made for me
the timing of which designed perfectly
but this Love, this Love here and now
this Love hurts
because she didn't Love me.

Blue Rose

A delicate flower grown from my dreams
With it its roots firmly planted in my heart,
God tendered the seed with
the golden liquid of life
and bright rays of His Glory
I did not notice at first
distracted with weeds, thorns, insects,
yellow lilies all around

But magically out of the corner of my eye
something begins to blossom
Never have I seen anything like it
I draw closer to it to examine its deposition
From the thorn-less stem spreads perfectly shaded blue pedals;
curves of a well-groomed rose,
lies the sweetest nectar within its center.

Only the purest of hearts of bees can reach
I desire not to pluck it from its placement in the ground as I'm afraid
I may damage it. So, I sit peacefully beside the majestic wonder as the
wind blows calmly between us. I simply and continuously smile at the
once upon a time unimaginable sight of the beautiful, magnificent blue
rose

The Yearning Heart

Heart yearns for another
but cannot find
seeks, cannot see
smell, cannot taste

In the distance, a spark appears
draws him nearer
blood rushing through the veins
pumping rapidly, excitingly

"What is this glimmer that I see"
closer brighter wider, light becomes
red jewel takes shape
a glow that matches the sun

His drum ceases to slow down
in his warmth, the jewel protectively held
breathe of life, it beats
without his eyes, he knows

Symmetric rhythm, they pump
symphony of the drums
walk side by side, toe in toe
seek, no more
found his other
hearts of two now one

You Are PT 2

The moment we met eyes, I knew

YOU ARE

The lift beneath my wings,
Carrying me higher than the stars,
and straight into the sun,
Burning hotter than the nuclear fusion that makes up its composition.

Falling to the Earth, cooled below the dew point of the moistened
cloud,
Drenched in precipitation of your God-loving secretion,
I walk across the solidarity of our relationship (you are my rock),
And over the threshold into your warming breast.

Drying me off in the security of your thumping chest,
I lay across your lap in complete comfort,
Listening to the lullabies of your words which is your voice
Total Bliss… this is where I would like to be for eternity.

The moment we met eyes; I knew you were mine

YOU ARE

The lift beneath my wings,
Carrying me higher than the stars,
And straight into the sun,
Burning hotter than the nuclear fusion that makes up its composition.
Falling to the Earth, cooled below the dew point of the moistened cloud,

Drenched in the precipitation of your delicate secretion,
I walk across the solid ground beneath, you are my foundation,
And over the threshold into your warming breast.

Drying me off in the security of your thumping chest,
I lay in comfort across your lap,
Listening to the lullabies of your words which is your voice
Total Bliss… this is where I would like to be, for an eternity.

The moment we met eyes; I knew you were mine to be

LOST AND ONLY YOU

I'M LOST
SOOO lost.
I mean, lost with no want to be found.

Lost in the sea of your eyes,
The crashing waves pushing me to depth's bottomless love
The sinking floor of confusion, popping out on the other side of the earth
only to find myself blinded.
Blinded by the mysterious mist of your aroma,
My internal compass out of whack,
Points not to magnetic fields of the north but directly to your chest.
As I walk towards your eternal peace of embrace,
Feel the gentle sands of your skin squishing between my toes.
Guided only by my memories of yesterday, today, and to come,
Each image with your shine radiating my day,
Seeking the sweet nectar only your lips can provide.
Drowning in the chocolate swirls of your hair
I'm overstuffed with your compassion,
Suffocating, I can't find my way back to the surface of sanity,
My body never to be found.

Do not take me from this place of forgetfulness.
Forever lost in you is where I'm meant to be.

ONLY YOU
It is only you that I know. From the dark shades beneath your eyes to the polished nails on your toes. The books you hover over in the midnight to sweet delights you crave during the day's light. The whispers of an annoying child that drives you insane to the loud screams of the trombone that makes you feel sane. Not a word spoken I know those desires without you even needing to mention. I know you better than I know myself. Not even a year have we spoken completely or been in the same vicinity, yet it is as if we never left. It seems we met in my mother's womb and that's where I got to know you. I know that may

have sounded creepy since this would make us siblings but it as if our blood was intertwined before time was even written. I know no one else or nothing else but you. These poems I write, I write only for you. You are my inspiration. Every stroke, pen scratch, and finish set to race to chase the inner chambers of your heart. It is all done for you. At last, if you only got to know me like I know you.

I SEE YOU TOO

Laying in the Color of Your Skin Tone. **T**he tiny brown specs that settled here to form this huge landmass **B**lended with the empty homes of once living seafaring creations of God **E**ngulfs me beneath its warm surface with nothing but my head as evidence that I still exist--**C**omforting embrace that only you can give **M**y entire body covered with minuscule particles of sand touching places that I cant even reach--**Y**our angelic gentle hands touching the hidden places of my soul **E**ncouraging me to do things I thought was impossible.

Looking Into the Colored Shades of Your Eyes. **T**he fluffy whites moving along in the blue heavens **S**hapes the face of pure beauty--**I**mages of the smile that cheers up the lowest of spirits **A**s the night owl reveals its shade **T**he bright stars glows of your presence into the dark **I**lluminating the deepest crevices of my core pushing me to go forth.

Listening to the Gospel Choir of Your Voice. **T**he harmonic waves crashing into the shoreline--**Y**our voice setting my heart into perfect rhythm. **T**he oceanic blasting winds whispering your name into my ear electrifying my very being into action.

Living in the Locket of Your Heart. **T**he ocean's perfume permeating through the moistened air--**Y**our sweet fragrance lifting me off my feet Leading me above the heavens **T**he cooling waters of salt--**Y**our surrounding presence calming the nerves within **T**asting the preserving salt of your love with every gulp of air.

My life My love, wish you were here standing side by side as One upon the endless sands merging into the flows of the sea but even when you're not in everything I do **I Only See You**

Every man has that person who inspires him to produce master pieces of art and reach their highest potential. Thanks for being my muse and inspiring this poem ;-)

WHY AM I THAT GIRL?

The question was raised,
why am I one of those girls?
and I simply responded,
some things are not explainable, indescribable, too pure to conceptualize,
words can't describe
but when I use the words, they do not fully capture the true meaning
of what I'm trying to say
the heart and soul of this unconditional feeling that does not make
sense but still I know it's there
a step below the heavens of the Highest emotion that God has for his
people that feeling that is beyond the human understanding and of the
purest form
the way you make me feel as if I can run the world and conquer it twice
over again
you get me beyond I know myself and let me be me even when I don't
like me
fill that void that is hard to reach with Him being the center piece
my thoughts connect with yours and disagreeable are easily swayed
when our sweet voice speaks about them
your conversations spark interest that are not easily discussed with
others
you challenge my train of thought and inspire me to be better than
what i am
you make me stronger and exceptional and wish not to fall from the
high of which you provide
as your beauty rise from the inward out it's hard not to stare at you and
see an angel before me that can't be match by any other
So be mine and don't let me go and as I attempt to hold tightly to your
heart and secure it within my own chest

The Attractive Force

The indescribable attractive force
the black hole light can't escape from
No matter how far I run
it calls, I come

Gravity that binds man to earth
with the sweet words, it sucks me in
then it has me pinned
a wrestling match I can't win

The heavenly power that holds our galaxy
moon rotates around the earth, earth can't leave the sun
the Godly substance that connects me to you
destined to be one before it's all said and done

My heart has no place to run
nowhere to hide
it seeks thee forever
as high as the highest mountain side
The lowest valley
deepest water depth
 without thy presence
 I cannot take a breathe

The magnetic force
 pulling North or South
 squeezing my lips to yours
performing mouth to mouth

Light Breeze when I'm around you
Cold harsh rain when I'm not
wind blowing east to west
moon pushing the tides

The empty vacuum of space
that sucks in all the air
you are stealing my heart
really isn't fair

But of this, I really don't care
because I rather be stuck to you like glue
while drowning in the deep blue
then be left living in this world without you

Letting Go

Why can't I let it go?
What is keeping me attached
stuck to this derailing track

This addictive drug
blood sucking bug
It has a hold on me
and won't let me free

God please help me
I don't know what to do
I'm sick,
the only healer is You

Stop this pain, this curse
release me of its purse
Logically it makes sense
just leave it alone
my heart easily overrides my dome

Everyone telling me
just stop, live better
it doesn't appreciate you
move on with your life
this isn't helping you
either way, I won't feel right
I try to remain calm
ughhhh!

I'm sick of this sickle-cell pain
But it feels so good
brief moments of ecstasy
so high it scares me
a glorious fantasy

Recapturing me,
back into its clutches
Telling me it still wants me
Playing games with my head
"Come back to me"
"I make you happy"
"I don't like you"
"Now leave me"
It just may kill me
if I don't let this free
a bird stuck in a cage
wishing to spread its wings

It says it doesn't mean to hurt
but oppositely
actions pushed
continuously
24/7 its calling me
To reach out to it
I can't
I won't
I shouldn't
No longer control me
manipulate, trick me
Push out of my mind
stop the updates
No more gifts
nothing from me you'll get
The tides have shift

It hurts to see
you be so carefree and happy
without me
but with him

Still, don't want to see thee
get hurt by him

so be careful
as you propel yourself upon him

No longer will I see
that smile of cheer
hear that ringtone
that excited my ear

Vision blocked of all you
to better me
heal me
Forever will I keep
those deep secrets
you hold so dear
never to be uttered
from my lips
so, don't you fear

Yet, a glimpse appears
of what could be
a future that should be
If only you wanted me
as much as I you
Loved me
cared, adored me
truly and honestly

Dedicated to us
exclusively
our intimacy
none in between
You just see me
no one else in the frame

You with me
feel not lonely
Dream of dreams

so patiently I wait
You find yourself
mature and grow
realize what you've done
miss me
then I'll come
It was meant to be

God's prophecy
not momentarily
but someday
However, this is reality
and now
it's just me

Completely free
no worries
"What's the lesson learned?"
I don't know my Lord
"everything will come to past
eventually
move on for now
and then you'll see"
easier said than done
Why can't I let this go?

She is my drug
that stole my thump
Attempt to make peace
I forgive thee
of all thy wrongful deeds
to set thy own self free

Essence

What is the essence of beauty?
Is it just the outside appearance of the things I see with my naked eye,
Or is it something much, much more?

It's that object deep within the very being
Rising outwardly to the physical formation of her curves
Expressed through the subtle actions she chooses to demonstrate to the
world.

First time your sugar brown eyes locked with mine
And I knew you were the one I wanted.

Character of those delicious plump lips
Showing off a straight line of pearly whites
Forming a genuine smile of honesty and purity.

That HUGE brain spitting out facts and figures
Yet creatively designing the soft harmonies of joy,
Your thoughts coming off in perfect pitch with mine.

Image of you petting a cute fury white rabbit
In the middle of a fresh green meadow.

It's the very God-fearing soul
That loves His Son and, in the end,
Wants nothing more than to please Him.

Your natural goodness
Radiating from that caramel skin
Warming up the room.

The mesh of our bodies melting together
Underneath each other's sweet embrace.

Making a spiritual contract with the instruments of our bodies
Under His watchful eye
As our souls intertwine into one.

It's the continuous outburst of laughter
Springing from the core
As we walk and talk.
But all of these are mere phrases describing one specific kind of beauty.
Then how can we know exactly what the essence of beauty really is?
We cannot except unto ourselves
And what it appears to be from our lonely view

Truly the essence of beauty is in the eyes of the beholder
I say, In my eyes
You Are True Beauty

P.S.
I look into your red rose heart
And I hope to see me
Cuz that's where I want to be.

The Flames of…

This mysterious red Flame
is hotter than the Sun's blazing core.

It scorches my heart,
consumes my being,
desires companionship,
and chases away reason.

Feed it devotion
to give strength
to the forever Flames.

Lust its igniter,
Passion its oxygen,
Trust, its wood.

Once lit,
It may descend to a low simmer,

But the Flames never diminish

SO, I CAN BE COMPLETE

You are God's gentle creation RIPPED from the cage that protects my
airway.
There's no way you were formed from this earthly flesh.
You are far superior than I could ever be.

Your juicy lips sweeter than the blackest berry

Your smell purer than a flower's gorgeous scent

Your hair more precious than golden silk

Your skin softer than a thousand feathers

Your voice more soothing than a heavenly orchestra

When you talk to me,
my heart thumps with ecstasy.
It hears the language of your heartbeat.
Be forever near me,
to fulfill the missing me.

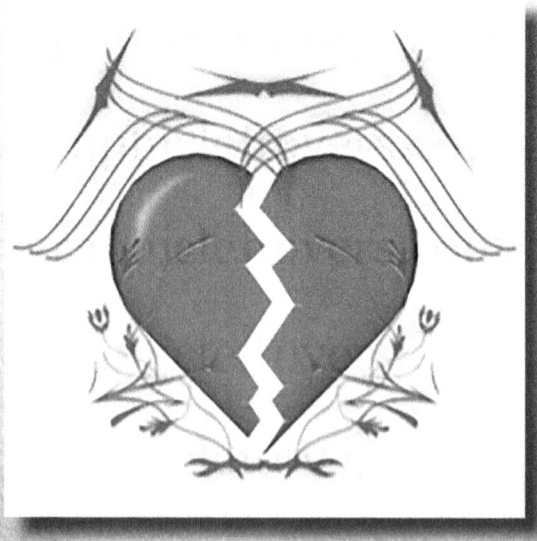

I NEED…MY WIFE…MY LUV

I NEED THEE.
all of thee.
not just a part of you
not just a nibble
but you, in its entirety.
Not the half-truth
no secrecies
but the whole and nothing but.
All the good, the bad, and the ugly
not all at once
but eventually,
over time,
every single bite.

I NEED TO
see you, in you, through you, even the glorious shape.
feel and touch you.
caress the parts that make you quiver with bliss
decipher your speech when you don't talk
fill the holes no other man is meant to touch
poke the inner crevices of your soul.
kiss you, hug you, luv you deeper like you've never been before
and you never will again.

I NEED YOU TO
place your smooth delicate skin against mine,
persuade my mood with your chocolate eyes,
press your succulent lips upon the tools of my speech,
lay your black Nigerian hair across my chest,
as we fall asleep to the gospel melodies.

correct me when the time is needed,
fight me in moments of stupid stubbornness,
wipe my tears during periods of sorrow,
surprise me on occasions of unexpected joy,
as we discover the gifts and coals of life.

I NEED, I WANT, I LUV YOU

I love everything about you
Every curve, piece of fat, wrinkle, and sagging part
You name it, I love it
Because it's you
It's you, to live, is what I need
It's you I want to be with
It's you the one I love

Hold the key to my heart now and into the days of old

I WANT YOU TO

understand my being,
yet willing to work through the confusion,
the frustration, the anger, the joy,
the anguish, the sadness, the blessings

I WANT YOU TO

sail on the white clouds with me
as I reach for the heavens
while you reach for the stars

I WANT

your heartbeat in sync with mine
to share my thoughts, my heart, my soul
with no one else but you and the Lord
oneness and perfect harmony

two spirits, two minds, two cores
me and you
connected as one
under the Trinity of the one Son

RED JEWEL

Its Red as the red rose
with the soul of a sweet black berry
Hair soft as the cool gentle breeze
Eyes that can calm the wildest beast
Sparkle brighter than the night sky
Lips sweet as the honey dew
Juicier than the juicy fruit.

It's soft as a lamb
Wise as a wolf
Humorous as a hyena
And strong as a bear.

Its skin is more gentle
And smoother than the best made silk
So warm it melts into my breast
Perfect within my arms
We become one
And everything is rite with the world
Rightfully in my hands
And me not wanting to let it go.

An irreplaceable ruby
Brighter than the rest
Forged from the depths of the earth
But found to be perfect and pure.

The only problem is
It's not my jewel to keep
Found on another's property
At a time when excavation wasn't welcomed.

All the proceeds go the owner
While I watch its beauty from a distance

Getting as close as I can
Without tilting the covered glass
Setting off the alarm
Getting harassed by the force.

I start to search and excavate
For other precious jewels
As I study and examine them
I can't find one that compares to The Jewel
But nothing compares to The Jewel
And all the while
I still wish I had
The Red Jewel.

TO AWAKEN TO ETERNAL BLISS

As sweet as the melodies are in Heaven is your shining light to my awakening soul... I thank God for waking me up this morning and smile as you lay beside me... It is because of Him that both have become my reality...

CHAPTER TWO

HEAVENLY MESSAGES

These next few poems speak to the struggles and triumphs of the Christian soul. The first poem is the theme of this entire book. I believe everyone has something to say in this world and rather or not you say it verbally, you are leaving a message and legacy for others to follow.

THE UNSPOKEN SERMON

Speak your unspoken sermon
Speak the words
That ears cannot hear
That the mouth can't say
That your actions can't even
Justifiably portray
Just live, be you,
And try to live God's way
And He'll be sure to
Listen to what you have to say

You have an audience around you
Every single day
Watching and waiting for
Your sermon of the day
Anticipating exactly what it is
You're going to say
Sure, you're going to mess up
And make a few grammar mistakes
But don't worry
God got spell check
And He won't let you fall off to far astray
He published a help book with everything you need

For you to read anytime of the day
He's not going to force you
To say anything His way
He's just going to sit back and watch
What it is you want to say
When you get home though
That's when He truly judges
Your life sermon of the day
Big Brother is also sitting
In the audience

Listening to what you say
He really smiles when
You proudly and boldly
Speak the things
He taught you to say

If you cry and get nervous
He's right there
Wanting to take the pain away
He encourages you and says,
"It's okay, the pain won't last always"

There will be critics
And those who mock you
When you pray
But the opinion that really matters
Is your Father's anyway

NAKED

Unclothed,
bare,
filth,
ashamed,
unhidden from Your wrath of Love.
Every scar,
scratch,
bruise,
You see me.

The imperfections of my feet,
as I stumble along the beaten path.
The crooked curves and twist
of thine soul,
blemished with the wages of death.
Spotted with the dirt of man all over.
You get me.

Every inch and fiber that covers my skin,
the count of each hair follicle,
abs a little too round,
gushing pimples filled with oily shadows of my desires,
the mark of birth upon my chest,
the rhythm of my heart pushing
sickened cells through clogged vessels,
You know me.

Scorned,
crippled by time's brutal waves,
burnt by the scorching sun of loved ones,
my back slashed with the Devil's lashes,
You heal me.
The blood stain cleaning the wretches of thine being.
Saved from the torture's depths beneath the surface.
You love me.

Thank You for the bath
with purity of the pierced side making me whole,
Clothed in the burdens of Your thorns,
access to shining Glory has been received
You and only You,
Rescued me,
Purged me from myself,
SET ME FREE!
Naked but not forgotten by Thy Son,
Forever in the presence of Eternal Joy.

A note to whom is imprisoning me:
I CHOOSE TO LIVE

I choose to live;
I do not know the definition of life,
the meaning of it,
or what exactly it is to be alive,
but I choose to live.

A tiny dot in a sea of darkness;
Who am I,
what am I,
these questions have yet to reveal themselves to me,
but I want to find out,
I want to live.

Trapped in this comforting fluid,
this flexible wall of warmth,
chained by this chord of bodily nutrition,
as soothing as this prison may be,
I wish to escape the confines of this space someday,
and I choose to live.

Blind to the world around me,
surrounded by sounds I yet do not understand,
if I knew how to pronounce the messages spoken beyond these walls,
I would say these words,
I choose to live.

I do not know what lies past this chamber,
who I belong to or what I look like?
what beauty and sorrow awaits me?
where I would be or where I would live?
but the one thing I do know,
I want to live.

Everyday more parts are added unto me,
touch more of my world,
reach further with any four of my new limbs,
use them to circle about and twist;
But my cell is growing smaller,
the time is nearing for my escapement,
I choose to explore the great beyond,
i choose to live.

Gracious by the means of which I came into existence,
beginning to recognize certain tones and volumes,
some to my liking and some not,
I wish to hear these same instruments on the outside,
I choose to live.

More and more senses are beginning to emerge,
with a heart that beats I feel,
pain of every rough bump,
joy at the blissful noises of the other world,
ever growing love for this thing called life,
I choose to live.

Finally, liberty,
Give me birth, lungs to breath,
with all my rights granted to me,
now my inexcusable death could cause you problems,
so, protect me, guide me, teach me, feed me,
AND-LET-ME-L-I-V-E-LIVE

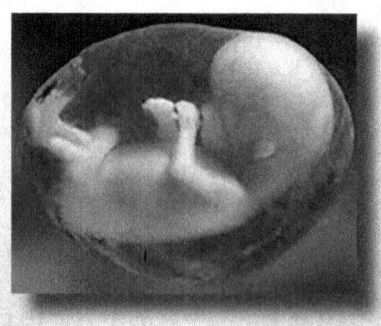

THE VALLEY OF SHADOWS

The Bare bark trees, can see the white of their bones
crooked pointy curves, sharp leafless branches stabbing the flesh at
every turn

the ground weighing me down not wanting to let me go
knee deep, thick muck of spit and brown sinking me further into its
mouth

surrounded in rich viscosity of smother upon which my lungs cannot
inhale
damping out any brightness that may exist beyond its mass

the sound of silence echoes through the passageways
I cannot even unmute the bellows of my own voice

I hear the stench aroma of death creeping up beside me from all
directions
The pungent touch of his tiny little hands crawling all over me

My mind rattles with the looming darkening of what could unfold
Yet my heart does not tremble

For a Man who walks above the bubbling earth treads beside me
His peace dwells within my inner being

The serpent's tongue cannot poison me
For the red sparkle of the Lamb runs through me

The tiny drips piercing from my skin wets the hole of His palm
Guiding my footsteps to the direction of serenity

Beyond the walls, the light breaketh through
Footprints not of my own, carry me to the journey's end

Afar the brief journey of this realm of shadows
Lies the forever slumbering palace of His goodness and mercy

O to THEE thy FATHER

I wake to abide in Thee,
hoping to be a better me;

The Spirit of Thine Love resides in me.
Teach me Your charity,
so that I may know how to be,
and share it with Thine offspring;

Teach me Your hate,
so, I may not stray,
and stay on the path that's straight.

Thank You for the Son;
the red coated Lamb,
taken with the Broken Bread,

Spring of Life spilling from Thine side,
now death has been overcome.

It is He that shed for me,
the Father wept for He,
but He wept for the one next to Thee.

The blue sky reveals Thine face,
gloriously shining beyond the vastness of space;

The pleasures of Thine grace,
awards me a heavenly place;

The river flows over my soul,
cleansing this diamonded coal.

Your beauty is all around me,
the yellow lilies, colored leaves from the Autumn trees,
winter's snow, covering the Poles,

the whispers of your voice in the breeze,
your volcanic screams, bursting with fiery justice,
this is all Your beauty.

I cry out to Thee,
when I can't see, which way to go;

Surrounded in smoke, I climb to breath,
mind filled with fog,
no light to be found, yet I knowth the surface is near,
but then, the ladder extends another eternity;
set me free, from this misery, O Father,
letting go, I fall,
behold, caught by the Grace,
the angel's wings catch me;

Above the darkened clouds we fly,
everything now seen with clarity,
feet set on firm solidarity, with Him.

Always taking care of me,
thank you Holy, for being with me,
all praises to the One and only King.

The nightly silent slumbers,
filled with lively wonders,
but in You, whom I must follow;

Your wonders for me, the mind must boggle.
Finally, tonight I slumber,
with Thine hovering Peace

THE CHESTED BIBLE

I hold my bible close to my chest tonight
Hoping to dream the thoughts of my master for my life.
He guides me through

Lead me and I shall follow You
Thank You for bringing me through.
All glory belongs to You.
Again, I say, thank You
Amen, only with You.

I wake up with its words embedded to my soul.
The day belongs to You

TIME and ETERNITY

I have been scarred by the grace of time.

Bruised by the sinner's stone. Battering waves crushed my soul and thrust me against the rigid boulders along the cliff. I've nearly drowned under life's flooding waters. Lost my bearing when the twisting whirlwinds came. Choked on the world's golden dust. Broke my legs falling into inescapable pits. My back shattered underneath the immense load of painful memories.

I cover my face to hide the shame and tears.

But, with the everlasting Word
my sins are covered by the majestic Christ. His rich healing blood flows through my veins. The living proof I am His kingship's heir. Loving raindrops of mercy provide nutrients for my wrecked soul. Sweet melodies of the cool gentle breeze soothe my heavy-laden mind. I hold tight to His firm hand as he pulls me out of the quicksand. The pure living water forever satisfies my thirst. His perfect compass points me back towards eternity. His warm glorious light dries my tears.

My face radiates with His love for all to see

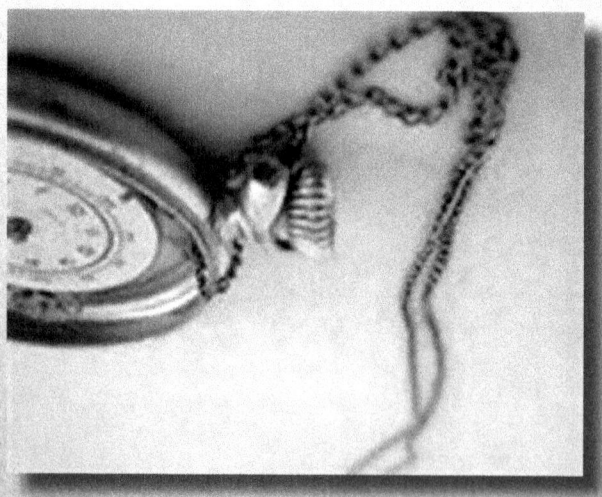

A PERSONAL THANK YOU
TO THE PERFECT EXAMPLE

Thank You Father for making me out of your beauty

J.C., Thank You for being strong so I can learn how to be

Your perfection is my guidance of how I should be

You, Holy Counselor, is wise beyond measure and

You know everything there is about me

God, You are Love

and that's what I'm trying to be

HEAVEN

We should all live comfortably and free
Each day in a place that is far, far away
A place called heaven
That is glowing always
Where the streets are gold and sparkled
And it's safe to play in them any day

There is a mansion at every door
And steps of the eyes galore
It's such a magnificent sight to see
Especially the boldness of our majesty

The almighty sits high
On his big wide throne
With His son on the right talking on the phone
And His best friend on the left laughing with His homes
With kings of crowns
Sitting all around Him
And four odd powerful creatures
Watchfully guarding Him

He's so big and vast
He's everywhere you are
The light that shines from Him
Is brighter than the morning star

Angels everywhere
Singing praises to His name
And glorified saints
Doing the same
No more pain or strife
Or troubles to worry about
Everybody is healed
And all that old stuff is out

So just relax and enjoy
And even boldly shout
Cuzz you're in heaven
There's nothing else to pout about

It's high above the earth
And past the known skies
It's way beyond
The stars and the moons
Its farther than our solar system
And beyond the universe rules
But if you want to get there
There is one thing you must do
You must accept J.C. as your Lord and Savior
And do as He say do

So, let's all try our best
While on this earth
To be the perfect Christians
God wants us to be
For the love of Christ
And heaven after death
Is where we should all want to be
With one physical death
And life for eternity

STRUGGLES

Beat up, Beat down, repeatedly
punched, kicked to the ground
the cement has become my friend

Dragged through the streets
brushes displayed for all to see
Jesus Christ where are you
when I need you to be?

Father, You are so cruel to me
lettings things unfold as they be
with no visible intervention from thee

"What doesn't kill makes you stronger"
repeated in the ear constantly
but the road to recovery
is much harder than the brutality

Wounds heal slowly
infection always a possibility
scars left to remind me

Mental memories haunt me
there seems to be no end to this misery

KILL ME NOW!
put my mind at peace
but wait, can't let the enemy beat me so easily

Continue to fight I must
for the few who believe in me

When I don't believe in myself
keep saying it
maybe it'll come true

"I can win this long, enduring battle
through Him who lives inside me."

SHORT SAYINGS

- This architecture built on the blank dark canvas of time laid out before my eyes is reason enough for me to believe.

- It is harder to act on one's beliefs than to merely state thy belief. The question then becomes can you be called a true believer if you can do one but not the other.

- A man's worth is measured by his actions and not merely by the words by which he speaks.

- The warming rays of Thy glory is why I praise Thee.

CHAPTER THREE

MILITARY LIFE

What is the true cost of being called a hero? The following explores this concept through personal experience and empathic observation.

EXCITEMENT

Never have I felt so high
Waiting for this chance since I was knee-high
Saying goodbye to the place that gave me so much grief
That opened my eyes to a whole new world
Opened doors and made me more bold
Taught me things I will forever hold

As I wait in anticipation
In the bullpen of friends
Dress in the impressive blue choking band
Here come the memories
Flooding back to me
The flip book of my personal diary

Friends I met along the way
Cherished stories told for another day
Lifelong mates forever by my side
Late nights, pick-ups, and knocked out teeth,
Laugh out loud
Thicker than blood brothers are why I love the academy
(Here's the table just to name a few
Shawn, Scott, Will, Troy, Jon, and T-Stew
Okezie the right hand brotha too
And the best roommate Lance Wu
Please don't be mad if I forgot to mention you
No disrespect, know I love you too)

Always remember the Tiger Ten Fam
That crazy band
of brothers and sisters
Then there's the baby redeye
Those who helped ease the sting
of freshmen year in my right eye

Alpha Squad at the prep
my first military pack
All the USAFA classmates and friends
Teachers, mentors, sponsors, and church fam

So much pain and agony
The basketball and mechie family
Day and night all there were
No sleep to finish the assignment due

But family it was
And the passions I loved
So Only the good I'll keep
And the rest into the ocean's deep
I made it through
that's all that count
Grateful, the blessings I count

Like the pink sunset
Flowing down into the evening sea
I glow a radiance the whole world can see
Waiting in the bullpen
They count us from one to ten
We start the final march of harmony
To the long blue line, we go
YES! It's time for the show to begin
In the tunnel of thin air, we roar
"HAAAP" from our thunderous core
On the plush green field where Falcon football is won
Today is our day to be the victorious one
The stands are full of everyone we love
The image of God's lovely dove

The President is here, is all the cheer
DVs announced and accolades gave

Honors to them for the way they paved
Speech made by the big man himself
The time is nearing to shine myself

This beauty you must see
A black man
Reaching out to the shake the right hand
Of the first man of brown skin in charge of liberty

Out of respect I saluted he
It was not for him or me
But the men who struggled for me
The men who struggled to allow him to hold that office
The men that gave me this opportunity
The men that made me
(Thank You Grandpa James, Grandpa Sam, Albert Wells, Dan, and many more)

The child like joy
Of playing with one's toys
Has spring up within
Jumping around in the playpen
Waiting to be picked up by the Thunderbird's wind
Diploma in hand
Waiting for the military man
To give his final command

"YOU--ARE--DIS-MISSED"
Jumping higher the tallest 10-foot man
Hat thrown WaaY above the stands
Hugs from the entire fam
Kisses and tears of unbelief
It's finally here, it finally happened
Lt Wells, you are a graduate!

Excitement
Of pure---absolute---overwhelming---heavenly---[Screaming]-
JOOOOOOY!

MY WAR

Mickey Mouse Club

Yelling, screaming, hours of physical mental exercise and pain
The first steps of indoctrination
The color of tradition kicks me in the rear telling me to shape up or
go home
The long blue line

Service before self, Excellence in all we do, Integrity first
The heart of the Wing, the Truth

The worm eats through the book of equations
as I learn disciplinary lessons of an officer
To be or not to be is the subject
If I sit in this chair will it break is the major

Five years of training
Year by year-gradual progression to normalcy

Graduation is the ultimate prize
The fighters flying by
Caps thrown high in the sky
Firm grip of the president's right hand
Diploma in leadership in the left

No more Mickey Mouse rules
The club days are over
Now the real adventure begins

Warheads on Foreheads

Let the bombs fly through the white clouds
Searching for the red dot
In a blink of an eye
the fearful terror meets their 40 virgins in heaven

Bullets fill my chest
blocking my airway

I watch my friend head get blown away into a million pieces
Blood gushing out of the shattered leg

The protective eye watching overhead
The frontline grateful for their presence
I order men to face the door of their Maker
Hopeful we won't meet Him until a later day
We fight on the topsoil graves
of the lifeless camouflaged bodies

A child picks up an abandoned toy car from the street
The attractive red device takes half her face
I stare into her cold dead eye
Deep within is man's attempt to recreate hell

"Today is your lucky day"
"Your papers just came in to go home"

Land of the Free

The shelter of refuge
Welcomed with open arms
The streets cheer as I walk down the lane

Respected by all
Forgotten by my family

"Who are you daddy"
"That's not how we do things, honey"
Where did my wife and life go
They left for another

"Don't call us, we'll call you"
I guess launching missiles is not a prized skill
Holding up the sign, "Will Work For Food"

Where are my brothers when I need them the most?
Help line, Help line please tell me what to do
The gun is in my hand and its ready to shoot

Through my new eyes, nothing is the same
Everyone is a suspect, must protect the red, white, and blue

Visions control my thoughts
Nightmares ruin my sleep
Old habits cause involuntary movements

I see her everyday
crying as the red fireflies screech across her face
A hole made through the source of the screams
The crying stops
It rings through my ears
as I stand in New York I visit my friend 22
His left leg is missing, his right arm too
His burnt lips attempt to smile
as I walk through the room
We laugh, we joke, we sob,
we reminisce the days
I wish I saw him more
during his last days
This is my brother
Bonded by the blood of others
What we did out there
kept us close to one another

Everything is not bright
Everyday isn't sunny
Normalcy isn't normal
That is the biggest change
Eventually, things will make sense again
But today—is not that day

This is truly my war
Now and forever more

A HERO'S FUNERAL

Hear the thundering blast and the burning bullet fly by, the constant reminder of the already fallen lay nearby. Render the final salute as the eyelids forever touch. The 26-gun salute roars through the ears with the grievance sounds of Taps. Reminded, "It is the soldier who salutes the flag, who serves beneath the flag, and whose coffin is draped by the flag..."[1]Ashes to ashes, Dust to dust, Back to the earth from whence we came. Goodbye my friend, Now my spiritual comrade. In your boots, I continue to march, until it's my heavenly release of the warring pain.

"A fallen United States soldier, airman, and midshipman is an unspoken hero of freedom"- Nathan A. Wells

1   Charles M. Province https://www.goodreads.com/quotes/235880-it-is-the-soldier-not-the-minister-who-has-given "It is the soldier..."

TO FLY

I want to fly high into the skies
Those beautiful heavenly skies
So blue and so true
Pure as the white dove crew
No, but as the single dove glowing
With the radiance of the Father's Love

Those wonderful merciless skies
That brings rain when everything is dried up
That brings the storm to clean up
Our mess after we've spilled the cup
Filled with man's sins and wrongful hook-ups

Laying on the ground
Looking at the clear blue skies
Watching the birds go by
Is not enough for me

Sitting on a cloud
Flying slowly by and by
Or flying so fast
That the birds are watching me go by

Blazing through the plows of clouds
Making streamlines
That you can see for miles

Be high as the listening skies
Listening to the musical wind blow by
So high where the birds can't even fly

Eating with my heavenly Father,
My crucified Brother and my Inspirational Friend
Talking about the wonders of the world

Touch the first heaven
Enter the second
And relax in the third
-Cloud Nine High-

Reach the place where dreams are made
Then the place where dreams are obtained

I want to fly
No, I'm going to fly
So, if you want to reach me
Just meet me in the sky!

High Flight
by John Glisby McGee Jr.

O, I have slipped the surly bonds of earth and danced the skies on laughter-slivered wings
Sunward I've climbed and joined the tumbling mirth of sun split clouds and done a hundred things you have not dreamed of
wheeled and soared and sung high into the sunlite silence
I've chased the shouting winds along and flung my eager craft through footless halls of air
up, up the long delirious burning blue
I've topped the windswept heights with easy grace where never lark nor even eagle flew
with silent lifting mind I've trod the high trespassed sanctity of space, put out my hand, and touch the face of God

This is my favorite poem about the beauty of flying and the reasons why the Air Force was created. I wrote my own version of what it means to soar in the skies in the poem previous to this one.

                                    - John Glisby McGee Jr., "High Flight"

THROUGH THE EYES OF A SOLDIER

Killing is wrong, and God said murder is a sin,
but war is inevitable & you must defend.

God sent his people out to defeat their enemies, but sometimes they
fought for land that God only promised them from infinity.

Is this right to take land from another because you feel it's your right?
"But God told me to do it", people proclaim to defend their so call
rights.

Only God can say who should live or die,
but if anybody else says it then it's a lie.

God spoke directly to his people when He told them to defend their
rights. But is it right for God to tell them to destroy who we see as
innocent life?

Don't get me wrong, I'm not saying God is contradicting Himself when
He said murder is wrong. But then He sent His people out to defend
like there was nothing wrong.

God ways aren't our ways. His thoughts are much higher than our own.
He sees things that we cannot see, & that makes our judgement wrong.

So, who are we to say that it was wrong when God told His people to
fight on yesterday. He did it so He can show His people His wonderful
ways, & who He is back then & today.

If God felt those people should be casted away, so His people can live
another & better day. Then only God has the right to say.

My heart ache though Father for Your not with us like You was on
yesterday. When a war breaks out and the world today, I don't know
which side is truly doing it Gods way.

But I have this humongous urge to fight you see, & it won't seem to let go of me.

To fight for my freedom & my family, my rights & my land. No matter what the cost I will fight & won't stop until it's all safe & free for the homeland.

But can I take another man's soul? The most precious & dearest item that every man has? The one & only item I can never give back?

It's not just a man's soul I took away. It's a little girl father, a grown man's brother, I just blew away.

Somebody important to somebody else, will not be returning home today.

BECAUSE OF ME! BECAUSE OF ME! because I had to take him away!

We, soldiers, try to convince ourselves "It's my job, it's something I had to do. Not because I wanted to, but because my country asked me to."

But when you out on the battlefield, you're not thinking about the states, the pride of your country, your family, or those stakes yo' mama fixed for you the other day.

All you think about is that band, that band of brothers facing the enemy, fighting with you, all trying to survive so that one day, we may all return to the homeland, completely safe someday.

When it comes down to it, all you see is that first enemy, but you can't pull the trigger. And if you shoot the other way, it's almost certain that you will be returning home, with honors on your casket that day.

So, you shoot! Bang! You stand there wondering, What Just Happened! and you finally realize, you just made a man's heart flattened!

You saw the man skin color, hair, & where he possibly came from. You even saw the color of the man's eyes, & deep into them you saw where the man soul lies.

You've just crossed the line, the blood line of death. The place of pleasure or eternal regret, but once you've crossed it, there's no turning back.

But now it seems easy, destroying da enemy, without any regret. For the thought of killing a man, isn't any longer a threat.

But you will always remember, remember your first kill of a man. That's the man, the one man, you will never forget.

Now your best friend has been shot & you don't know what to do. The war becomes personnel, you want to destroy the enemy too, for what he did to you.

They took your brother's life away, & that wasn't fair. He was just trying to survive this evil warfare.

You hate the enemy now. You want him gone. You want him out of your sight because he sent your brother on home. So, to get pay back for your friends' death. You try to release as many of the enemy souls as you possible can, also hoping you might pay off your own debt.

Despite the negative effects, & the worst possible outcome, that is sure to come for most. I still have this urge to fight, & fight for something with worth.

I believe in my country, I believe in its success, I believe in my family, my freedom, & that we are blessed.

War will always be out there. There will be people trying to put us at an end. But there must be a soldier. Who is willing to defend? So, I will fight until the very end, for my rights & homeland security.

For I am a soldier, who has a strong desire to fight. One who is willing to do anything, to make sure the homeland is alright.

But if I die on the battlefield, just know that God knows best, & He decided I needed to leave, & put my soul forever at rest.

CHAPTER FOUR

LESSONS & MEMORIES

These speak the different life lessons I have learned and cherished memories that have stuck with me.

SLEEPLESS NIGHT

Heavy eyelids shutting out the light,
Tiny needles pointing at the joints,
Wet rug drenched with the burdens of the day, too hefty to pick up,
Yet fail to visualize the fantasies of the night.

The shattered heart of a love which I caused steady pounding on my
frontal lobe,
I try to fix the fragile pieces with nonstick glue,
What should I do? Cuz I don't have a clue,
The guilt, the shame, the smell of hunger on the tip of the tongue.

Why did I do this, who am I? the bite of a gnarling wolf,
Sharp razor teeth penetrating the skin deep down to the red pump,
Peace is what I desire, not this strife,
This harmful deed I commenced, paying the price of the sin.

Lord, lead me back to the warm breast of the one I dismayed,
And no more will I ever bear my fangs and press them upon her neck.

JUST A NICKEL AND A DIME

"Don't give me 15 cents, just a nickel and a dime"
Midnight Jerry
Knees on the wooden floor
Nightly cries to the Almighty
50 years of stewardship to her side
Daily love spats in their old age
Midday news [slash] midday nap.

Early morning rise before the roster even cried
Chopping wood, tending the garden, feeding the stock
A farmer's work is never done
Born into a world of Jim Crow
Sufferer of pain so his children wouldn't have to
Never stopped loving a brother from another mother.

Bold, strong-minded, persistent, and independent
Countryman, warrior, World War II vet
A man of enormous wealth
Wealth of a caring family
Uncles and aunts, nephews and nieces, children, grand and great
Friends from every place he stepped.

A few straight silver hairs covering the source of his knowledge
A skinny belly, "I love me some fish; I'm trying to be as big as you"
Enduring muscular arms squeezing you tightly into a great gubbly gue
Big long hand teaching a young man how to use his
Pushing the next to reach higher heights
Strong stick kept him walking on the righteousness of his faith
Dark leather skin to weather the storms.

"I don't want 15 cents, just a nickel and a dime"
That's what he used to say
Before the sun rose, he rose
With a fresh pot of coffee and a washed face he went out

Went out to the fields of the day, wherever the fields may be, and
worked
Everyday
Every day he worked.

He worked to provide
To provide for his household whomever lied within
Provide a home full of love, food to feed the belly,
knowledge to handle the random, skills to accomplish the task,
toughness to go out-conquer your dreams,
best example of servitude he could be as a mere man.

Rest now from your toils and long days of work
Be blessed with the mate of your soul
I cry a tear for your absence,
a prayer for your travels,
and a shout of joy for your happiness
I will love others as you have loved me
And I promise to continue to climb,
climb the ladder of my dreams.

My Grandpa
Grandpa James Smith

THE SNOW-COVERED MOUNTAIN
(EVERY MAN IS THE MOUNTAIN)

The mountain face covered in unique snowflakes.
Purity of the whiteness blankets the landscape,
Not a blemish of freckled soil to be found upon its face.

The sun rises, the face turns into the very substance God made every
man from.
The texture that has no bounds when seen only with the naked eye.
The enriched essence of the variant shades of caramel sprinkled all over
as the groundwork for life to come.
Springtime comes around, face no longer the color of the ground, no
more brown.
Green grass run wild, tall tress stretch out their luscious lavender leaves.
Yellow lilies and velvet roses blossom their glory for all to see.

Falls turns around, leaves transform to brown, orange, pink, and red.
They fall to the floor; a child's masterpiece of a handful of crayons
smeared on a blank canvas.
God's abstract art.

Deep down within its chest,
Lies a beating heart of bright cherry-red coals whose heat is only
exceeded by the sun.
Smoldering rocks that liquefies anything in its path;
fumes from it pointed noise during moments of great frustration.

The wintered white snow claims the face's edges once again. But it burns with the red fiery within all year long only to bleed the same.

WHEN THE SUN SAYS HELLO, BUT THE SHADOWS SAYS BYE

When the rays say hi and moon says goodbye,
the birds sing songs of praise to the Highest,
and thank Him for the new day...

When the sun says goodbye and the moon says hello,
the cricket whispers a lullaby,
inviting you to close your eyes,
and rest the weary night away...

The Sun rises,
stretches out it's shiny rays far and wide,
brightens up a big yawn for all to see,
says goodbye to the glooming moon,
hugs the earth,
giving birth to the great lands of mass and animals from their slumber,
brings life to the freshly scented flowers,
warms the hearts of God's special creatures,
Shake Thee humble servants and says,
"Let's begin, it's going to be a good one!"

MY BROTHER

There is no other
Mainly because you my only blood brother
Thicker than water, born of the same mother

Looked after me since you were five years old
I still hear all the stories you told

I farted in the tub, but it felt kind of weird
Next thing you know, daddy orders a clean-up of the tub and my rear

You've been cleaning me up ever since then
Even when I frustrated you again and again

I wanted to be like you on the court
So, you offered your support

But I whined, complained, and didn't want to practice
You grew angry and weary but never restless

I ran home crying, wishing I were better
You kept pushing me, believing I could do whatever

Set an example I found hard to follow
Little Daniel became my name, a name I learned to swallow
Talent, excellence, hard work is what was expected
Determination, respect, God-fearing in me the experience effected

Good minister, friend you have been
Tough love, soft hugs; you used to help me win

This game of life has proven to be difficult
I hurt, squeeze me tight, pouring tears are the result

Together we've seen a lot
Katrina and death, for me, is the heartache plot

We fought; we laughed, and shared many beds
Making this relationship as strong as good woven threads

We've taken the same events and made them our own
And into myself I have grown

Creating differences on in this life
Yet still talking to you is like knife sharpening knife

Much more to learn from each other
Congrats on finding your significant other
I love you my brother

THE BEAUTY OF SOUND

Poetic lyrics recited over rumbling rocks
of bangs and booms.

Sweet melodies glistening
off the gentle flowing stream.

Miniature angles chirping
God's heavenly gospels.

The first cry of a baby heard
from the rose pedaled squeaking bed.

Roaster crows the morning alarm.
Carbonated pressure released
from the cold beer can.

The cows moo and the wolf howls
as they sit beside the crackling fire
on the countryside hill.

Stand on the snow-covered mountain top,
gentle wind whooshes in your ear,
tickle feeling of moisture covers your whole body,
fills you up with excitement,

bursts out of the mouth as a yell,
echoes Helloooo, throughout the cravens,
lava explodes from the volcano.
Head bobs, hands go up,
waving back and forth.

Hands clap, hair flings,
panties swoosh through the air.

Bodies jump up and down,
building shakes and rumbles.

Rockets flare up,
fireworks sparking.

Detonations in the skyline,
lighting up the nightline.

Feet stomps the wooden church floor,
low monotone hymns buzz the air,
claims of the Holy Ghost cause many to go mad.

Surround sound noise,
honking cars, fussy neighbors.

Pianos falling from roof tops,
dog barking at the roaring thunder.

Shhh, complete, silence;
sitting on the front porch.

Creek, creek the rocking chair says;
z off to the kids playing in the yard.

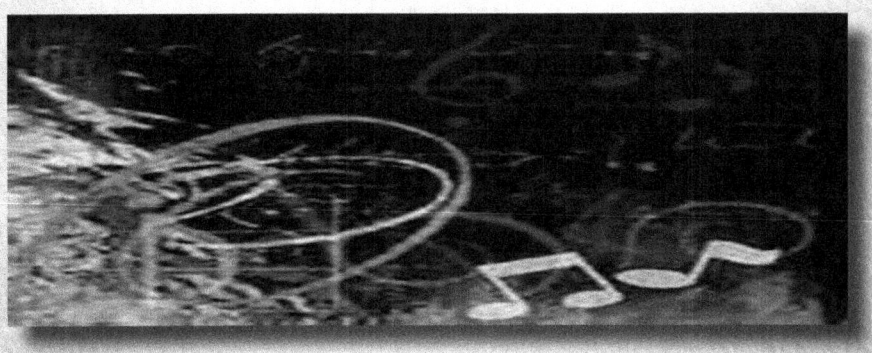

AN APPLE-SEED DREAM

The Apple-seed's dream
to be the biggest tree

nestled in apple core
protective layers of cozy-warmth

hangs from branch
sucks nutrients from Mother-tree

falls gently to soft ground
aged leaves purposely placed by her

squirrel eats apple
Apple-seed breaks free

poop less stinky
settles in better ground

room to grow
enough sunlight

forms own veins
grows one leaf above surface

--older Trees protection--
secured higher ground

less floods
blocked winds

took on fires
stabilized earthquakes
fought hurricanes
battled snowstorms

terrified lumberjacks
--shook away lighting- -

years pass by
not as many scars

branches thick and wide
veins sturdy and strong

leaves are delicious green
apple-seeds of his own

taller than any Tree in the forest
bigger than any Tree before him

dream came true
bared less heartache

suffered less pain
seen different adversities

still struggled
made it through

made his time his own
Lays his leaves down for the next great Apple-seed

WHO AM I…TO DEFER A DREAM?

Who am I… to not continue a legacy--
my parents have set before me
Who am I to not work hard--
my ancestors have worked more diligently
Who am I… to not take advantage of--
seek after the opportunities--
my elders struggled to acquire?

For little ole me,
they've done this and much more,

so, pursue my dreams I must,
as they are inside me,

pushing me…to move forward,
farther than they ever hoped.

I am their living memories,
I am them,
They are me.

---LANGSTON HUGHES POEM "A Dream Deferred"

"What happens to a dream deferred?
Does it dry up
Like a raisin in the sun?
Or fester like a sore--
And then run?
Does it stink like rotten meat?
Or crust and sugar over--
Like a syrupy sweet?

Maybe it just sags
Like a heavy load.

Or does it explode?"

STILL DISTANT

Distant from the womb of birth
firm hand of guidance
wrinkly hands of love
presence of a forever annoyance
abuse of brotherly hugs
houses of care

Separated from my Chocolate City
the rich culture
its historic memories
aroma of deep sea on my plate
soft, harsh melodies
season of green, purple, and gold
hang from the magnolia tree
the beloved saints of old

Pushed away from my youth
b-ball and football played on the asphalt
quick pause in the game to let the car pass
long pedal rides in the neighborhood
discovering new places to trespass
the little kid's school

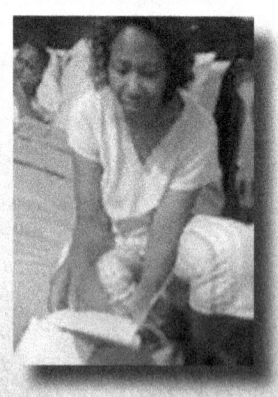

Kindergartener's nap time
an A in every class
imaginary hoops played on poles
the golden saxophone as my instrument
the rainbow belts from karate
evenings at Tee Dee Dee's house
childhood playmates
since 10 months old
Uncle Mike's whip whooping our hides
--my nonblood related family

Taken from the yellow buses-
lethargic drives under early morning clouds
-one hour per mile-
the muggy heat
deep within the clouds is the sun's smile
illusion of the cool shadow tree
soaked with sweat before the day even starts
waiting for the bell to ring
encircled golden mustang on the white polo
days in the education complex
the freedom of the lunch hour
converse with the peers
broken unprotected fence kept us locked in
young love built and crumpled in a day
popularity checked and secured
manhood tested on the cracked courtyard
playing with banged up hoops

football shattering bones on the dusty grass
the athletic bonds of the pigskin crossing the goal line
friendships made through harsh practice
the teenager's journey

Driven from the sanctuary
the old and young mixed into one
deacons and church mothers
the kitchen's southern scents
sisters and brothers
weekday youth programs

Wednesday's bible study
Thursday's choir rehearsal
Saturday's activities
Sunday school lessons
wisdom shared
traditions taught
slave songs riveting the room
the forever Spirit
wavering fans
high shouting hands
loud halleluiahs
the never-ending message

Removed from Orleans Parish
tourists, wild parties
Bourbon Street
Essence Festival
don't forget the zoo
where they all ask for you
Audubon Zoo
east beast
your ward
the projects
Hot Boi
bounce music
Who dat…dem Saints
Second Line
the Big Easy
The Bowl

Why was my car pushed into nature's washer machine?
my b-ball floating down stream?
why did I never return
to the empty city?
Why did I choose this path?
clothed in blue integrity,
sacrifice and liberty

1,000 miles away
chasing my dreams
or is it?
it chose me.

God chose it.
Who chose what?
my destiny
Why am I still so far?
far away from the rocking chair of nursery?
gone spiritually
disconnected from the tragedy,
physically
yet it stills haunts me

Is this where I want to be?
not representing the black and gold jersey
with people of familiarity?
but this is where I need to be
for my family
for me

Katrina took part of me
never to return
so, make do with what you have
and let the rest burn

Perfect for me
these difficulties
challenge me
strengthen me
like a skyscraper
higher and higher He builds me
I'm here now
the Academy
and forward where I must go
zooming in the fly machine, F-16

check your six
but take only a glance
too long of a stare
and you'll be caught in its trance

But I'm still distant
away from the southern hospitality
the jazzy melody
the N O soul of
the boot shaped state
now it's not the same
and it never will be
she has forever changed me

In your hearts of hearts
as sweet lemonade
shall the past always be
yearning to be free

So, let it go
and express it where you are
don't be afraid to be you
plus, more of who you are

WHAT DO YOU SEE? (AGE 17)

When I look at me, I see,
A beautiful handsome young man,
A young man trying to become a strong black man,
Perfection in progress.

A young man trying to grow in wisdom,
intelligence,
And in God's love.

A young man trying to exemplify Christ,
In everything he does.

A young man trying to respect and love everybody,
Just as much as he loves himself.

That's what I see,
When I look at me,
Now, the question is,
What do you see?

GRANDMA

I don't have any grandmas
yet I have three
they are no longer here
but forever they exist in memory
their souls are now in heaven
but they live also within me

I will always miss them physically
but I shall stay carrying them spirituality
they passed on down to me
Jesus, thank you for allowing me to spend time with them
but I am also glad they are now in heaven's eternity

God Bless you
Grandma Clare, Helen, and Kayretha
Miss and love you always
Your son
Nathan Veal Smith Wells

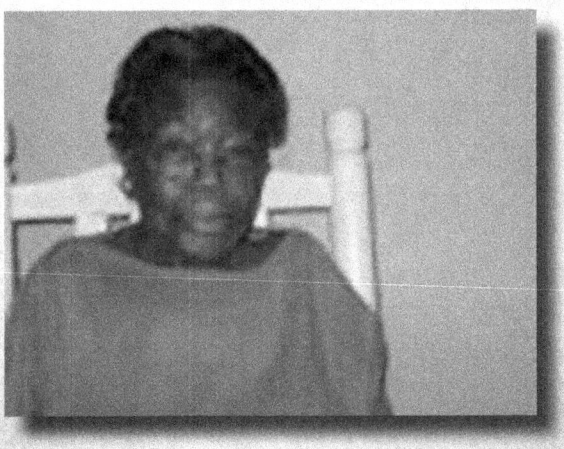

MAN OF YOUR WORD

The only things you are left with at the end of the day is your word, your respect, and your reputation.

For fear, money, and power are forms of respect, but doesn't necessarily bring true respect.

Respect for you and not what you have, but what you do for them or do to them.

A man of his word keeps his word. He doesn't lie, use disrespectful words, or does anything to compromise his word.

Your actions are confirmations of what you say. So, say what you mean and mean what you say.

That's your word,

For your word is a bond, a commitment to your actions of what you said.

If you lie, no one will trust you.

If you verbally hurt people, no one will want to be around you.

If you disrespect yourself and your word, then no one else will love you.

Not even you.

Leave your word at the table.

Don't say you're going to fly when all your doing is sitting on the ground watching the plane go by.

Choose your words carefully,

and do as He say.

Be a man of your word and of His Word,

and don't be a fake,

cuzz someday the only thing people will remember you as is who you were,

and not what you pretended to be.

So be a Man,

and keep YOUR WORD.

CHAPTER FIVE

SHORT STORIES

A collection poetic stories for the mind and soul

SINCERELY, SMILEY

Hey Old Man,
I'm writing this final letter to say thanks.
Thank you for your presence.
Hot summers and watermelon seeds.
Wintertime and a fire to feed.
For being a grandfather of love and care
Showing me God's love by loving thy neighbor as thyself
Calling a man of opposite color your brother
A stranger your instant friend
Future wives as daughters/husbands as sons
A beloved uncle as a close companion until his end.

Thanks.
Thanks for teaching a young man how to fish
Catching a baby fish, throw it back to find its mother fish
Chopping wood,
setting fires,
checking under the car hood,
how to drive back to MS from Terry, MS
Staying active through the years
Calling, "Hey Smiley I'm so glad to hear from you.
Terry boo and Suzie Sue called too.
Got up this morning,
went to the gardens before the sun woke up and caught wind.
I have some peas and potatoes coming in nicely.
Now I'm in the house watching 9 AM news at 9 o'clock precisely."

Thanks for being strong and living long.

The things you've seen.
The historic stories told that enriched my soul.
For wearing the uniform,
the battles you fought for our victory.
Struggling to provide in the harsh racial countryside.

Teaching your children how to strive, for excellence.
I stand on your shoulders now brave and bold.

Thanks for praising the Most High.
Then loving your family with ultimate pride.
Displaying true love from young to old.
Now you can be with her in the heavenly skies.
Crying when your hurt showing me that there is nothing wrong with me.
Big hugs, "mmmhmm, great guebubbly gue, O I'm glad to see you".
Praying on your knees that rumbled through the beams, Of the aged home.

So much more I could say,
in my heart will the memories stay.
This is my farewell for now,
until I'm called to my earthly end.
Always loved.

Sincerely,
Smiley

THE LETTERS – WEEKEND OF A LIFETIME

Late night, meeting my date in person only for the 3rd time. She patiently waits five hours for my arrival. Ironically, it is the same location when we met for the very first time. Happy to see her gorgeous smile as we meet, talk, chat, and wait for the pick-up from one of my dearest friends. Explore the base/university I call USAFA. New experiences and sites to see for the young lady whereas I grow weary of looking at the same ol' thing. Tick tock, tick tock, the clock calls us to move forward. Getting fresh is an art which I strive to perfect every day. Cleaner than you have ever seen me in a uniform that only comes out on the rarest of occasions. DAMN! Babe, you look some good in that fly ass dress. I play it off real smooth and cool like. Let us go up top to the T-zo and let the world see this beautiful black dynamic duo in action. Snapshots and camera phones, professional cadets, and friendly requests, smiles and cheers all around. 1,2,3 pose! A thousand times over. Unbelievable happiness runs down my face. The ceremonies begin. Friends all over, toast and speeches, skits and memories be made, military formal dining in traditions commences in full swing. Dinner is served. Who spent the most? Who just met their date? Ridiculous USAFA run by ridiculous cadets. Finally, the moment I've been waiting for. That beautiful 14k white gold surrounded in bubbly champagne. One kiss for practice. Down the hatchet it goes. Soft succulent lips extract the prized possession out of my mouth. And there it is. Class crest, white diamond synthetic stone, grown man sized handle, squadron patch-10-once tiger always a tiger, "Work Hard, Hard Work," Nathan Beanie Alexander Wells forever inscribed—the symbol of all my toils and tears, successes and failures, happy and exciting moments, unforgettable friendships at the United States Air Force Academy easily placed on my finger. Aww. A perfect match to my slim figure hands. Now let the real festivities begin. Over to Henry "Haaap" Arnold's dancing hall. Mostly greet and meet as the music plays. Look at that huge ass cake! Free beer. Yes, thank you kindly. I will take one. Mad rush to get to the party bus before it takes off. The engine starts and off to Breckinridge we go. All my buddies under one roof. Crazy loud music. Liquor in one hand and beer in the other. Trying to dance in the confined space. Oooo that booty feels some good on top of my lap. Necessary stops every 30 minutes extending the two-hour drive even longer. Excuse me bus driver, sir, my bladder is about to explode. Crazy people making small little puddles with their bodily fluids all around the innocent helpless gas station. Red, white, and blue lights flash in the air. "Party ON" Mr. Po-po says. Raging throughout the night, day, and night again. Hot tubes with snow falling from above, liquor and booze only, no food to speak of in the fridge, music and wild dancing, shouts and screams, straight shot from whole handles gone within an hour's time, everyone having extreme fun to say the least. O, an exclusive room just for my date and I for the entire weekend. You guys are too kind. The overly drunk, the under drunk, the sickly drunk (nasty), and the just right let's party all night. Snow on the mountain tops. Delicious crepes to seal the morning cravings. Lovely ladies taking care of their idiot male counterparts in the evenings. Stories only to be retold among friends for years to come. What an expensive weekend this was but what an experience I'll never forget! Ring Dance was Awesome. Time to get back to Florida. Goodbye my date. Thanks for coming. Later USAFA. See you in a week's time. See you my dudes. Only one year left. Let us make the most of it. All man, what a weekend!

THE LETTERS – FERL OPS

Two weeks spent in Florida—Hurlburt, Duke, Tyndall, Eglin AFB/ Pensacola, Dustin, Fort Walton, Panama City Beaches

Tiny bubbles of warmth from the bright yellow rays. Laying on layers upon layers of microscopic white crystals. Salty waves crashing on the shoreline. Making splashes as I play and swim in the greenish blue. Making sure to not swim too far into the ever-growing deeper waters. Shouts of laughter spring from the sandy courts as I attempt to play the silly game of volleyball. Up and down it bounces from hand to hand. Jumping near the nets. Spike. Oopps. That's a point. Thank you. First time gamer. Barely making it over the net. Most times not at all. Sorry. My bad. Game continuous with no time limit. No points just fun. Ball busting collisions between teammates. Growing more and more proficient in the act of the game. Game becomes more competitive yet just as fun all the same. Enjoying a nice cold one. Looking past the long leg-studded pier and into half of the yellow-reddish and pink glow of the sun as the earth conceals it for the night. Listening to the wondrous orchestra of the birds' chirps, roaring waves, soft breeze, joyfulness from kids and adults alike, and hitting of the ball. Deep into the gulf, visuals of dolphins flipping and speeding through the waters with excitement as they put on a show for their customers. Riding on top of waves as we jet full speed on the two-seater water motorcycles. Getting splashed by salty H2O in the face. Screams of laughter as a fellow member falls off. Loving the company provided by my mom and sis as we cruised through the cold humid gulf on the "Sea Blaster". Hanging with my fellow USAFA mates as we eat, drive along, and enjoy the scenes the orange growing state has to offer. Jetting over the waters in my lonesome yet as happy as I can be, hitting waves and getting mad air. Summing up the adventure with prufoolery and dancing the night away with intoxicating excitement. Back to the Springs we go within a couple of hours.

Dirt boys and structures. Electricians and power pro. The CE world is a wonderful and vast place to be. Engineering at its best.

Seeing my years of studying coming to life. Setting explosives and charges. 3,2,1 Boom! Shockwave shivers my whole body. Air is filled with astounding mixture of gun powder and demolished dirt. The dangers of getting fried by the electric current. Controls operating the mechanical hands with precision, accuracy, and superhuman strength. Fires and emergency handled by the finest firefighters this country has to offer. Readiness keeping us prepared for what's to come. Chemical agents detected and protected by those who knows their dangers best. Heavy and hot suits for all varieties of protection. Thousands of pieces of equipment used for everything under the sun. So many things to know and learn, cannot possibly capture it all. The difficult task of leading experts trained in the duty of defending this nation through the mastery in specific technical skills. Decisions, decisions, what kind of officer should I choose to be. Flying above the ground God laid out for us, oooo, does this really row my boat? Hovers and cargo, big defenders, and offenders, what magnificent tools of the sky. Whole section dedicated to defending the home borders of the vast blue studded with white clouds. From the top to the bottom, CE is large and wide. Lesson learned from the Colonel -Ask not what the Air Force can do for me but what can I do for it. Air, space, and cyberspace- one part of our nation's great defenders.

THE LETTERS – THE ILLNESS

Hey again, it's been a couple of weeks since we last spoke, and you haven't responded to my last letter yet. But nevertheless, I will continue to write these letters until the summer ends. Hope you enjoy them as I re-live my experiences and share my thoughts and feelings in these summer letters.

The first night at FERL. I feel fine until I lay down for the night. In the small open space, shotgun shelter called a hooch, there were nine laid out dark green cots with 3-piece camouflage sleeping bags on top of them, two fans, four windows, and some shelves. My bunk mates start heading off to bed and turn off the lights. I bundle up in my protective covering as best I can, but it fails me. I shiver beneath the zippers. Initially, I blamed it on the Rocky Mountain chills of the night. The very dreadful air that I loathe and hate. Give me a reason to just quit everything and run back to the stuffy consistent heat of the south. As the night progresses, I close my eyes, but my mind refuses to slumber. Twisting and turning, my body cannot find peace or comfort. Hot and cold, on and off, hot, and cold. I find myself soaked in my own sweat. The nightmare is intertwined with reality. No distinction between the imaginations of my mind and the reality of life God designed. The two worlds merge into one. Caught between them like the vortex leading to the Twilight Zone. Finally, day breaks. More exhausted now than when I attempted to lay my head to rest. But the day must begin and there's work to be done. Continue through the day I will with all the strength I have left and hope for a more uneventful time later tonight.

What to do. It's been weeks since we talked. But every second we do not is like a stab to the heart. I know you said don't call again but I'll seek thee till the bitter end. Every day without you is hunger without food. Please forgive me for my past sins. Let us reconcile and make amends. I promise to never hurt you like that again. Just please let me back in. You are it. There is no one else. No moving on. Other girls I fancy and may have deep emotions for. But you are the one I cherish, and my soul yearns for. I dream of thy beauty, thy smile, and all that thou are. I do not know what to do without you being my center star. We were made for each other. Ordained by the heavenly Creator. Look deep into my eyes and you will see its truth. But you already know it for yourself deep down in your root. So please accept my appeal. Heal me of this illness with your love as the only curing pill.

THE LETTERS – THE TROUBLED HEART

Problems with the heart. Time heals hurt and pain. But True Love never dissipates. Brain tells thumb machine what to do. The lively red vessel ignores its commands and does what it wants. Argues with the brain over control of the body's movements. Brain struggles with the job of decision making. Headaches raised by the increased blood pressure. The heart wants to do the tango but the desired partner refuses. Stuck wanting more but the prize is too far out of reach. An ornament of passion and commitment. The heart knows what it wants, begs, urges, drools for it. The brain pursues and pushes for those wishes. ideals forever stuck and implanted never to be washed away. There is a thin line between love and hate. Back and forth I cross. Ultimately, Love prevails. Choosing to act in its best interest, preserve the rest of my beaten down heart and worn out brain. Blood flow traffic clogged up by the wreck. Clean up crew slow to react. Steadily the flow eventually gets through. To maintain peace and chivalry. Escape it all, briefly. That I must. Leaves doors open for a whatever future. Get back to me, I will… But you, forever a treasure. A chapter turned that redefines me. A new product of myself with added features is released. Thank you. if we never again meet, I am glad we met.

I WAS SPOILED GROWING UP

One day, my sis said to me that we were privileged growing up. That was not the first time I heard a statement like that because quit some years before that TDD (my aunt; Eunice Griffin) said that I was spoiled with a huge smile on her face. She had a smile of joy and happiness which perplexed me. If you are a hard worker like me, you would have been quick to reply with a 'No I'm not; I work hard for my achievements. I wasn't raised with a golden spoon' in my mouth. But this initial thought is blurred. I was not looking at the full picture or the context by which they were saying it. Yeah sure, we had good middle-class money but that is not entirely what they meant. My brother, sister, and I had two good parents that loved each other and us. A mom who cooked, worked, and did her best as a mother, and a dad who worked his hardest and did his best as a father. We have an awesome extended family. Two sets of grandparents that displayed 50 years of the ultimate love for their spouse and treated each grandchild as if he or she was the most special person in the world. Aunts and uncles that exemplified what it means to be good people trying to live in a battered world. Cousins that are always there for each other. A church family that raised me in the teachings of Christ and the proper way to live one's life. Close family friends that kept us and watched over us when my parents could not. Close friends from as young as toddler years that I still consider to be my brothers and sisters. Teachers, coaches, and counselors that forced us to work hard to make us into better people during their allotted time. We went to good schools (schools that were good by New Orleans, La standards that is). We were surrounded by everyday role models/heroes that guided, taught, disciplined, pushed, and loved us. We had a village of people that were dedicated to properly raising us the best way they knew how into fine young men and women. This is why I made it thus far. Therefore, I am who I am and why I have the ability and obligation to do so much before I pass on through this world. It really does take a village to raise a child. So now if someone asked me if I was spoiled or told me that I was really privileged in my youth, I would proudly say, "Yes, I Was". I was spoiled with love and privileged to have witnessed and experienced such dedication and love from so many people. I couldn't have asked for a better way or place to grow up in. My youth and the village that made it was my foundation with Christ as the corner stone. Thank you, Lord, for the real blessings in life.

THE SMALL THINGS

We never notice the small things until they are gone. We cherish them the most when we notice they are not there anymore and there is no way to get them back. Then and only then do we remember the simple gestures, words, expressions, and the tiny details that helped shape our current persona. We hold them tight to our memories and recapture how those special things made us feel when it was in our possession.

Amazingly, I remember the tiniest acts Mrs. Karytha Smith did when I was with her. I can vividly remember her sitting there in the middle of the living room with her mildly unstable mind and deteriorating, sagging body. Her back is hunched as she stares blankly into space and struggles to keep her somewhat bowed head up. She folds her arms neatly in her lap as she faces the front door while her back faces the TV. The only thing she seems to notice is her measuring cup she uses as a spit jar, her towel to wipe her mouth, and sometimes our voice as we ever so often tell her to sit up and hold her head back. As I sit there on the love seat couch to the left of her watching TV, I turn my head and grow saddened that her mind and body shifted to this horrible state. All the while, happiness also stirs inside me as I take in the fact that I'm glad to still be able to sit next to this wonderful amazing woman; this beautiful goddess who has soft brown skin and thin black angle-like hair that helped take care of me since my newborn days. The person I call Grandma.

For a moment I turn my head to look at her, she catches me looking at her out of the corner of her eye. She turns her head ever so slightly towards me. Her wrinkly face looks like it wants to smile but can't, but her crimpled old left eye purposefully, slowly winks directly at me! I smile and wink back, pleased and joyful to know she was able to remember the one small thing she and I shared. The special wink she gave me whenever her and my grandpa jokingly argued over whose grandchild I was or whenever she directed a special comment towards me. My grandpa would scream across the rooms, "You my boy. I'm going to kip-nap you and have you living up here with me." Then she would yell back, "No, you my boy, aren't you?" She would usually end the dispute by whispering to me, "You my baby," and then secretly wink at me. I would just smile and wink back. She would usually go back finishing whatever she was doing. This time after she winked though, she returned to the dead-look position she was in before, but deep inside I was overjoyed despite that her mind is slowly breaking down she had surprisingly decided to wink at me. Without even saying a word, I knew the simple gesture meant she still loved me. She still believed I was something special, and that I will always be her baby.

Of course, we always notice and try to remember the big important things, but we must never forget the little things and what they mean to us. I will never forget that wink my grandma gave to me, and I will cherish it as one of my finest memories of her, for I will never be able to see her wink at me again. My only wish is that we really notice and appreciate the small things sooner before they are taken away from us and will no longer be visible to us again. I love you Grandma and I'll miss you. Live free in heaven.

THE END

Hope you enjoyed. Thanks for reading.

INDEX

www.ingramcontent.com/pod-product-compliance
Lightning Source LLC
Chambersburg PA
CBHW060323130626
46553CB00003B/892

* 9 7 9 8 8 9 3 3 0 7 9 7 9 *